Take Up the

and Walk on Water

JUDITH ELMER

Copyright © 2015 Authored by Judith Elmer
All rights reserved.

ISBN: 1508447349
ISBN 13: 9781508447344
Library of Congress Control Number: 2015902408
CreateSpace Independent Publishing Platform,
North Charleston, South Carolina

Dedication

This book is written to bring honor and glory to Jesus Christ.

*This is my story, this is my song,
praising my Savior all the day long;
this is my story, this is my song,
praising my Savior all the day long.*

Song: "Blessed Assurance"

Contents

Introduction 1

The Shattered Hallelujah 3

The Battle Cry 7

Walk on Water 12

Why Look to Jesus? Who Is He? 16

A Call to Praise 21

Standing Firm 46

One Tiny Tick of the Clock 50

Seven Days of Praise 53

Appendix 63
All scriptures are taken from the New International Version (NIV) of the Holy Bible.

Introduction

I waited patiently for the LORD;
he turned to me and heard my cry.
He lifted me out of the slimy pit,
out of the mud and mire;
he set my feet on a rock
and gave me a firm place to stand.
He put a new song in my mouth,
a hymn of praise to our God.
Many will see and fear
and put their trust in the LORD.
(Ps. 40:1-3)

"God help me. God help me. God help me." That was the prayer my husband, Carl, cried out to God the afternoon he had a brain bleed and a massive stroke. After hearing my husband's cry to God and seeing the pain he was in, I immediately called 911. He was rushed to the hospital for brain surgery to relieve the bleeding.

The following is the news I received after his surgery: "A piece of your husband's skull was removed to allow for swelling and was placed into his abdominal area for safekeeping. In about six weeks, if all goes well, the bone will be placed back into his skull. He's on a respirator to help him breathe and a feeding tube for nourishment. The right side of his body is paralyzed."

Needless to say, I was numb. In a matter of minutes, my life had drastically changed. This was a storm. No, this was a hurricane! I felt like I was in deep water…over my head…and I was about to drown. I remember crying out to God saying, "This is too big for me. I need you, Lord Jesus. Help me!"

God heard both of our prayers. He heard Carl's cry for help, and God began to lift him *out of the slimy pit, out of the mud and mire (Ps. 40:2)*. And God heard my cry for help *and gave me a firm place to stand. He put a new song in my mouth, a hymn of praise to our God (Ps. 40:2-3)*.

This book is about the power of praising God for who He is and is a call for you to praise Him. Even when we experience intense suffering—whether it's physical, emotional, or mental—we can walk in His power and strength when we keep our eyes on Jesus. My reason for sharing my true story about taking up the praise is so that...*Many will see and fear and put their trust in the* LORD *(Ps. 40:3)*. The power of God is released as we praise Jesus. His power enables us to live life way beyond our own capabilities, in His strength and peace. When we find ourselves in life's stormy waters and we feel like we're drowning, we can rise above the deep waters of suffering and trials. Praising God through Jesus Christ gives us that firm place to stand so that we can "walk on water." Therefore, I encourage you to choose to take your position and take up the praise!

Turn your eyes upon Jesus,
look full in His wonderful face,
and the things of earth
will grow strangely dim
in the light of His glory and grace.

Song: "Turn Your Eyes Upon Jesus"

The Shattered Hallelujah

Though the fig tree does not bud and there are no grapes on the vines, though the olive crop fails and the fields produce no food, though there are no sheep in the pen and no cattle in the stalls, yet I will rejoice in the LORD, *I will be joyful in God my Savior.*
(Hab. 3:17-18)

For me, crying is highly contagious, especially when my husband cries. We've cried a lot since he had his brain bleed and stroke.

When you've lost so much and you feel shattered and broken,
crying comes easy.
When the struggle goes longer than you had ever expected,
crying comes easy.
When disappointment and pain stare you in the face,
crying comes easy.

Yet, even in those days when you feel there's no way you could praise God...you can! It's called a sacrifice of praise or the shattered hallelujah. *Through Jesus, therefore, let us continually offer to God a sacrifice of praise— the fruit of lips that confess his name (Heb. 13:15).*

A sacrifice of praise means to willfully "turn your eyes upon Jesus," even in our suffering. This kind of praise involves humbly coming before God with empty hands in a spirit of submission. We bow to God's way and God's timing. Submission is an important component of praise. Letting go of our control and surrendering to God's way and timing is powerful. Our shattered hallelujahs touch the very heart of God as we praise Him in our suffering. A shattered hallelujah ushers in the great blessing of God's peace.

I remember when God poured His peace over me. After seeing Carl's condition after his brain bleed and stroke, my heart was broken. I knew that what was happening to him, as well as to me, was way beyond our control. I felt like I had stepped into deep, stormy waters, and the waves were crashing over me. I felt weak and broken. I literally opened my hands and said, "Take this, God. You are Sovereign. I bow to You. Make good come from this, in Jesus's name." I knew that God heard my shattered hallelujah because of the calmness and peace I felt. God used the truth of His Word in Revelation 19:6 to remind me that He was in control and was the Winner—"*Hallelujah! For our Lord God Almighty reigns.*"

The truth of God's Word has the power to change you, encourage you, convict you, guide you, and comfort you. The Holy Bible is God's voice and His will for us. The Word of God can restore a sense of well-being, even during intense trials. Faith in Jesus and belief in the truth found in the Bible is powerful praise. Proclaiming the truth about God can change the way we think and feel. The shattered hallelujah that brings healing and peace is through Jesus Christ and the power of His Word.

> Even though I don't understand…You are Trustworthy.
> *But I trust in you, O LORD; I say, "You are my God."*
> *(Ps. 31:14)*

> Even though this feels too hard…You are my Strength.
> *I can do everything through him who gives me strength.*
> *(Phil. 4:13)*

> Even though things are falling apart…You are Sovereign.
> *He is before all things, and in him all things hold together.*
> *(Col. 1:17)*

> Even though my heart is broken…You are my Care-Giver.
> *Cast all your anxiety on him because he cares for you.*
> *(1 Pet. 5:7)*

> Even though this hurts…You are still Good.
> *And we know that in all things God works for the good of those who love him,*
> *who have been called according to his purpose.*
> *(Rom. 8:28)*

> Even though I want You to hurry…You are the Timekeeper.
> *There is a time for everything, and a season for every activity under heaven.*
> *(Eccles. 3:1)*

Even though I'm scared and You feel far away...You are Near.
Yet I am always with you; you hold me by my right hand.
(Ps. 73:23)

The shattered hallelujah comes from broken people. Brokenness is really a good thing. People who are broken are like clay in the hands of God, the Master Potter. If the clay is pliable and yields to the potter's hands, then the clay can actually rest in the hands of the potter. So, too, as God shapes and molds our lives, He invites us to rest in His hands as He holds and carries us. The Master Potter is shaping and molding me as He teaches me to trust Him without boundaries. When we yield to His hands and offer our shattered hallelujahs, we can expect to be blessed with His peace.

What is the Master Potter teaching you as He shapes and molds your life?
_____
_____
_____
_____
_____

Tell God how you're feeling.

_____
_____
_____
_____
_____

Now, take up the praise and complete this sentence. Father God, You are still…

_____
_____
_____
_____
_____

The Battle Cry

I waited patiently for the LORD; he turned to me and heard my cry.
(Ps. 40:1)

Have you ever felt like you're in a battle? I mean, where you find yourself in a storm, and your battle cry sounds something like...
The emotional pain is too deep.
My strength is fading.
I'm afraid.
This is taking too long.
Why is this happening?
Help me, Jesus!

A battle cry that ends with a call for Jesus to help is never ignored. He hears your battle cry. Jesus understands the suffering that ignites the battle cry. He cares about your emotional, mental, and physical well-being.

I like to think of the battle cry as a call for help. My husband's battle cry was simply, "God help me." God answered Carl's battle cry for help the night of his brain bleed and stroke. I stood amazed as I watched God orchestrate His help through first responders, the ambulance driver, the traffic, the doctors, the nurses, our immediate family, and our church family.

My battle cry was, "I need You, Lord Jesus. Help me!" Without a doubt, His help was evident. I remember the emergency room doctor saying, "Mrs. Elmer, your husband needs a neurosurgeon NOW." I answered, "I don't know a neurosurgeon." My pastor put his hand on my shoulder and began to pray. He simply prayed, "God, we need the BEST neurosurgeon for Carl. We ask this in the name of Jesus." Upon arriving at another hospital prepared to meet Carl's need for brain surgery, I was greeted by a nurse who said, "Mrs. Elmer, the best neurosurgeon is on call tonight." When I heard those words, I knew God had heard my battle cry. God was already ahead of us fighting the battle. I encourage you to pray big prayers! God loves to do the impossible, because then people will say, "Only God could do that!" I'm still praising God for being Sovereign over all circumstances.

It's evident throughout the Bible that God's people were not exempt from suffering. I'm sure God's people sounded their battle cries for help. Moses certainly experienced emotional and mental suffering when he was dealing with the grumbling Israelites. Noah and his family had to feel the pain of confinement inside the ark with all those animals. Daniel for sure suffered in the lion's den. The apostle Paul was in prison, shipwrecked, and beaten. I can't imagine the battle cry that Mary, the mother of Jesus, called out as she saw her Precious Jesus dying on the cross. Jesus Himself sounded the battle cry as He hung on the cross for the sins of the world…"My God, my God, why have you forsaken me?" (Matt. 27:46).

Jesus endured suffering throughout His life. He's described in Isaiah 53 as a Suffering Servant. Yet at the same time, Jesus was able to experience joy and peace even as a Suffering Servant.

- Jesus enjoyed being with children. *(Matt. 19:13-14)*
- Fishing with the disciples had to be fun. *(Luke 5:5-7)*
- Jesus was invited to weddings. *(John 2:2)*
- He enjoyed eating with friends. *(Luke 24:40-43)*
- He looked forward to His time of prayer with the Father. *(Mark 1:35)*
- I believe He had some good laughs with His disciples. *(Matt. 7:9-10)*
- Jesus sang too. *(Matt. 26:30)*

How Jesus lived is an example for us to live life in the moment—one step at a time, one day at a time. Thankfulness is a necessary ingredient for living life in the moment. Jesus modeled for us the importance of having a thankful heart even in the middle of major trouble.

Jesus had a thankful heart even knowing that crucifixion was ahead.

The Lord Jesus, on the night he was betrayed, took bread, and when he had given thanks, he broke it and said, "This is my body, which is for you; do this in remembrance of me."
(1 Cor. 11:23-24)

Jesus had a thankful heart even knowing that raising Lazarus from the dead would escalate the plot to kill Him.

So they took away the stone. Then Jesus looked up and said, "Father, I thank you that you have heard me."
(John 11:41)

A thankful heart can change our battle cries into shattered hallelujahs. Deliberately choosing to be thankful can change the way you think and feel. It's true that what we think about influences how we feel. Changing the focus of our thinking from worries to prayers of thanksgiving ushers in the peace of God. *Do not be anxious about anything, but in everything, by prayer and petition, with thanksgiving, present your requests to God. And the peace of God, which transcends all understanding, will guard your hearts and your minds in Christ Jesus (Phil. 4:6-7).* Changing the focus of our thinking from worries to prayers of thanksgiving really helps us to live life in the moment, one step at a time, one day at a time. Intentionally being thankful for the little things in life, as well as the big things, serves as a catalyst to praise. Many times throughout the Bible, we are encouraged to be thankful and remember.

Give thanks to the LORD, call on his name;
make known among the nations what he has done.
(1 Chron. 16:8)

Remember the wonders he has done, his miracles,
and the judgments he pronounced.
(1 Chron. 16:12)

I want to always remember that God saved Carl's life from the brain bleed and stroke. I'm so thankful. I praise God for being the Great Healer. Throughout Carl's recovering process, I've seen in many ways the healing hand of God.

The enemy tries to use suffering to drown out our praise; he likes to keep us looking at our problems. That's all the more reason to look up and praise God with raised voices, no matter how we're feeling. God knows how our thoughts affect our feelings. Our thought patterns change when we intentionally let our minds dwell on Jesus. God's Word, as found in Philippians 4:8, is an exhortation to think about... *whatever is true, whatever is noble, whatever is right, whatever is pure, whatever is lovely, whatever is admirable—if anything is excellent or praiseworthy—think about such things.* God wants others to see that when we shift our focus from suffering to praise, there's joy!

As we praise God, we are reminded that no matter what we're going through, God stays the same. God doesn't change. In the Old Testament, a long time ago, God led His people through the desert during times of intense hardships. *By day the LORD went ahead of them in a pillar of cloud to guide them on their way and by night in a pillar of fire to give them light, so that they could travel by day or night (Exod. 13:21).* Today He will do the same. He is able to hold you, carry you, and lead you through the tough times. He's with you all the way. He is still God and worthy of our praise. God is Good...period. Therefore, we choose to be courageous and take up the praise. In the name of Jesus, the enemy will not drown out our praise with suffering. Instead, may our praise be heard over the battle cry!

> *Accompanied by trumpets, cymbals and other instruments,*
> *they raised their voices in praise to the LORD and sang:*
> *"He is good; his love endures forever."(2 Chron. 5:13)*

What is your battle cry for help?
_____
_____
_____
_____
_____

What are you thankful for?
_____
_____
_____
_____
_____

God is Good…period. Praise Him.
_____
_____
_____
_____
_____

Walk on Water

Stand firm in the faith.
(1 Cor. 16:13)

To "walk on water" is an expression describing the Christ-given ability to still have the peace and love of God in your heart during intense times of suffering and loss. To walk on water is to walk by faith with Jesus. Looking to Jesus and trusting Him enables you to live life way beyond your own capabilities. His supernatural power comes from trusting in Him and Him alone. With Him we can rise above the crashing waves of life. We can stand strong and have a sense of well-being right in the middle of life's raging storms.

We live in a broken world. Some people have experienced...

the loss of a job,
a broken marriage,
the death of loved ones,
abuse,
the loss of health,
the loss of their homes,
and even persecution.

Yet some people courageously rise above their circumstances and...

still smile,
still have the peace and love of God in their hearts,
still believe that God is Good,
still give thanks,
and still praise Jesus!

That's walking on water!

How do those people do that? How do you walk on water? A requirement for walking on water is to…

"turn your eyes upon Jesus"
with an attitude of submission.

To turn your eyes upon Jesus is to choose to look to Him and not at your circumstances. It's a choice to draw closer to Him. In so doing, your love for Him can deepen. As your love deepens, your faith is strengthened, and it becomes easier to trust Him.

God has given us five major ways to draw closer and walk with Jesus.

1. Studying the Bible: The Bible tells us how to live by the truth of His Word.
2. Praying: Spending time with Him daily deepens the relationship.
3. Taking part in Christian fellowship: We need each other for encouragement and accountability.
4. Taking up the praise: Proclaiming the attributes of God and declaring that He is bigger than our problems brings about change.
5. Having a thankful heart: Remembering what God has done and remembering our many blessings can draw us closer to Him.

To humbly submit your control of a situation and give the control to God escorts in the peace of God. I experienced that peace the night of Carl's emergency brain surgery. I remember falling to my knees, surrendering, and giving my husband to God. I knew the peace I was feeling was supernatural and not something I could muster up. I was walking on water. The Lord is teaching me the power of surrendering throughout this long period of Carl's recovery. Letting go of self-reliance, money, strength, and whatever else we're holding onto makes room for God to be first. This is not to say that we're not to use our intelligence and supportive resources. Yet looking to God FIRST and not looking to ourselves puts God in the number one position to help. Making His will more important than our will ushers in God's peace along with His best plan for us. God ALWAYS has our best interests in mind. *"For I know the plans I have for you," declares the LORD, "plans to prosper you and not to harm you, plans to give you hope and a future" (Jer. 29:11).*

God's Word gives us a powerful lesson about walking on water. God used Peter's experience of literally walking on water to teach us some important lessons in life. The apostle Peter is one of my favorite people in the Bible. Peter was impulsive yet passionate and courageous.

"Lord, if it's you," Peter replied, "tell me to come to you on the water." "Come," he said. Then Peter got down out of the boat, walked on the water and came toward Jesus. But when he saw the wind, he was afraid and, beginning to sink, cried out, "Lord, save me!" Immediately Jesus reached out his hand and caught him.
(Matt. 14:28-31)

Jesus said, "Come," and Peter got out of the boat to be with Jesus. Walking on water was not Peter's reason for getting out of the boat. Jesus was Peter's priority. Peter was able to walk on water as he looked to Jesus and walked step by step toward Him. Peter was able to do the humanly impossible. But all too quickly, Peter's eyes went to the wind and waves. Looking now at his situation, he became scared and began to sink. Sometimes when our personal storms are raging, we can lose sight of Jesus, but He never loses sight of us. Jesus knows where we are every second. He knows what we're going through. As Peter's eyes went to the wind and waves, he yelled, *"Lord, save me!"* Jesus *immediately* (I love the word immediately) and without hesitation extended His hand and saved Peter from going under.

Peter was a devoted follower of Jesus. He had been with Jesus and had seen Him do miraculous things. Yet when the wind and waves got stronger, his faith weakened. What's so awesome is that when the winds calmed down and the storm was over... *Then those who were in the boat worshiped him, saying, "Truly you are the Son of God" (Matt. 14:33)*. God used the storm to strengthen Peter's faith. God uses the storms in our lives to strengthen our faith too. Our faith gets stronger as we look to Jesus, persevere, and trust in Him. I bet you could hear those disciples taking up the praise way down the lake. The storm was over, and the very Son of God was in their boat!

I can surely identify with that scriptural passage about Peter walking on water. Throughout this difficult season of my life, I have experienced Jesus's saving hand pulling me through. I, too, have been frightened by the stormy waves. Even the stormy winds, representing the things I can't see, tried to push me under. But as Peter showed us, when we call on Jesus, He is quick to help us. I'm thanking Jesus for the many times *He reached down from on high and took hold of me; he drew me out of deep waters (Ps. 18:16)*. The lifelong lesson

God is teaching me and showing me is that it's not about my strength to hold onto Him. Instead, it's daily trusting Jesus's powerful hand that enables me to rest in His grip.

Therefore, because God is Faithful no matter how deep the water gets or how strong the wind blows, by an act of your will, choose to take up the praise and look to Jesus. Get ready to rise above the storm and walk on water with His peace. Expect and watch for the blessings of His presence in your situation.

Turn your eyes upon Jesus,
look full in His wonderful face,
and the things of earth
will grow strangely dim
in the light of His glory and grace.

Song: "Turn Your Eyes Upon Jesus"

Describe a time when you felt as if Jesus reached out His hand and kept you from going under.

_____
_____
_____
_____
_____

Are you willing to get out of the comfort of your "boat" and come closer to Jesus? Explain your response.

_____
_____
_____
_____
_____

Why Look to Jesus? Who Is He?

But my eyes are fixed on you, O Sovereign LORD.
(Ps. 141:8)

It's impossible for me to adequately describe the greatness of Jesus. No one can completely describe God. Fortunately we have the inspired Word of God, along with accounts of eyewitnesses who saw Jesus, walked with Him, and followed Him to answer the question… "Who is He?"

The apostle John describes Jesus as
…*the Righteous One. He is the atoning sacrifice for our sins, and not only for ours but also for the sins of the whole world. (1 John 2:1-2)*

The apostle Matthew recorded that Peter said Jesus is
…*"the Christ, the Son of the living God."*
(Matt. 16:16)

The apostle Paul gives an account of Jesus's sovereignty over all.
He has authority even over death, satan, nature, and diseases.
Therefore God exalted him to the highest place and gave him the name that is above every name, that at the name of Jesus every knee should bow, in heaven and on earth and under the earth, and every tongue confess that Jesus Christ is Lord, to the glory of God the Father. (Phil. 2:9-11)

No matter how lengthy a description of Jesus is, it should always end with the words "and more!" His distinguishing nature is…
Loving *(1 John 4:16)*
Forgiving *(Ps. 86:5)*
Powerful *(2 Chron. 20:6)*
Compassionate *(Ps. 103:8)*
Patient *(2 Pet. 3:9)*
Comforting *(2 Cor. 1:3-4)*
Truthful *(John 14:6)*

Faithful *(Ps. 145:13)*
Steady *(Heb. 13:8)*
Transforming *(2 Cor. 5:17)*
Watchful *(Prov. 15:3)*
and more!

The inspired Word of God tells us that Jesus is…

The Gate
"I am the gate; whoever enters through me will be saved." (John 10:9)

The Light of the World
When Jesus spoke again to the people, he said, "I am the light of the world. Whoever follows me will never walk in darkness, but will have the light of life." (John 8:12)

The Good Shepherd
"I am the good shepherd. The good shepherd lays down his life for the sheep." (John 10:11)

The Way and the Truth and the Life
Jesus answered, "I am the way and the truth and the life. No one comes to the Father except through me." (John 14:6)

The Resurrection and the Life
Jesus said to her, "I am the resurrection and the life. He who believes in me will live, even though he dies." (John 11:25)

The Bread of Life
Then Jesus declared, "I am the bread of life. He who comes to me will never go hungry, and he who believes in me will never be thirsty." (John 6:35)

The True Vine
"I am the vine; you are the branches. If a man remains in me and I in him, he will bear much fruit; apart from me you can do nothing." (John 15:5)

Praise that pleases God is through Jesus Christ. *Through Jesus, therefore, let us continually offer to God a sacrifice of praise—the fruit of lips that confess his name (Heb. 13:15).* Through Jesus, we offer to God our praise. Jesus is the One and Only worthy of all our praise throughout all eternity. He is...

Savior *(Acts 4:12)*
Lord *(Ps. 136:3)*
Healer *(Ps. 147:3)*
Deliverer *(2 Sam. 22:1-2)*
Sovereign God *(2 Sam. 7:22)*
Immanuel *(Matt. 1:23)*
Creator *(Gen. 1:1)*
King *(John 18:37)*
Spirit of Truth *(John 16:13-14)*
Great I AM *(Exod. 3:14-15)*
Protector *(Ps. 91:14)*
One and Only *(John 3:16)*
and more!

Why look to Jesus? He is Faithful and True. He loves us so much that He willingly answered Father God's call to come to earth and take the penalty for our sins. *"For God so loved the world that he gave his one and only Son, that whoever believes in him shall not perish but have eternal life" (John 3:16).* God is Holy. Our sinful natures separate us from God. Jesus is God's plan for us to be together with Him forever. God's unmerited and merciful gift of grace is freely given to all those who accept Jesus as their Lord and Savior. God requires that we place our faith in His Son, Jesus, and agree to turn from our sin and to follow Jesus all the days of our lives. Jesus is the Only One who grants us peace with God. When we place our faith in Jesus, eternal life is secure, and God is pleased! *And without faith it is impossible to please God... (Heb. 11:6).* Jesus is the door to walk through in order to live forever with God.

Why look to Jesus? He came as a baby and as a humble servant and lived a sinless life. He died for your sins and my sins. His love for us kept Him on the cross. He died a horrible death by crucifixion. But death couldn't hold Him. On the third day, the tomb where they laid Him was empty! He rose from the dead. He's the Only One able to raise Himself from the dead. He now sits at the right hand of the Father in heaven. He's alive!

Why look to Jesus? He loves you. He longs to see you smile. His love for you is everlasting, unfailing, and unconditional. His love is deep, steady, and strong. He wants you to be with Him, to spend eternity with Him, and to enjoy the place He has prepared for you in heaven. But we can't get to heaven on our own. Turning from our sins and placing our faith in Jesus as Savior and Lord of our lives secures this wonderful place in heaven. *"Salvation is found in no one else, for there is no other name under heaven given to men by which we must be saved"* (Acts 4:12).

More good news is that we don't have to wait to get to heaven to experience a life overflowing with joy and peace. Right now we can have joy and peace, no matter how deep the hurt or how intense the struggle. In John 10:10, Jesus said, *"I have come that they may have life, and have it to the full."* I have come to realize that life "to the full" doesn't mean a life free from suffering. Instead, life "to the full" is a life lived in God's spiritual blessings. Jesus so willingly wants to bless us now with…

> the joy of His presence,
> the depth of His love,
> the power of His forgiveness,
> the strength of His peace,
> the blessings of His guidance,
> and even more!

Having a personal relationship with Jesus changes us. The power of His Holy Spirit enables us to achieve things beyond what we could do for ourselves. His presence strengthens us, sustains us, corrects us, guides us, and comforts us. God's free and undeserved grace given through Jesus is our hope. Victory over sin and death is ours through Jesus Christ. Wow! That's reason enough for you and me to look to Jesus.

Do you have a personal relationship with Jesus? Where you spend eternity depends on your answer to that question. If your answer is no or that you're not sure but you want a personal relationship with Jesus…

> Come as you are and accept His grace.
> Agree with God about your sins.
> Choose to turn away from those sins.
> Place your faith in Jesus.

Believe Jesus died for your sins.
He rose from the dead, and He's alive today.
Choose to trust Him.
Grow to know Him more.
Follow Him all the days of your life.

If you gave your heart to Jesus, His Holy Spirit lives within you. I encourage you to become involved in a Bible study to get to know more and more about the One who loves you for all eternity. Our love for Him deepens the more we get to know Him. The more we know Him, the easier it is to trust Him. Trusting Him strengthens our faith and helps us to be obedient followers. Therefore, *Let us fix our eyes on Jesus, the author and perfecter of our faith, who for the joy set before him endured the cross, scorning its shame, and sat down at the right hand of the throne of God (Heb. 12:2).*

How would you answer the following questions?
Why look to Jesus?
_____
_____
_____
_____
_____

Who is He?
_____
_____
_____
_____
_____

A Call to Praise

I will praise you, O LORD, with all my heart;
I will tell of all your wonders.
I will be glad and rejoice in you;
I will sing praise to your name,
O Most High.
(Ps. 9:1-2)

This book is a call to praise God in the good days and in the not-so-good days. Why? Because God's Word says, *For great is the LORD and most worthy of praise* (1 Chron. 16:25).

It's much easier for me to praise God in those good days when…

the sun's shining,
the doctor's report is good,
there's food in the refrigerator,
the kids are healthy,
I'm feeling rested,
I'm looking at the ocean,
I'm rejoicing over answered prayer,
I'm experiencing the comfort of safe travels,
or a baby was born.

It's much harder for me to praise God on those not-so-good days when…
it's gray and gloomy outside,
the doctor's report comes back saying my friend has cancer,
I've got to go to the grocery store again,
the kids are sick,
I'm exhausted,
I'm looking at all the dirty laundry,
I'm waiting on what seems to be an unanswered prayer,
I'm in the middle of a traffic jam,
or I hear news that a baby is struggling for its life.

Praising God is a choice. It's an act of our will whereby we choose to look to God and not to ourselves or at our situations. We intentionally choose to focus on who God is and on His blessings, no matter what we're going through. To praise doesn't mean that we're smiling and happy about our situations. Instead, praise is declaring the truth and insisting that God is Good…period. The truth about who God is enables us to rest in His hands, regardless of our circumstances.

No matter what…

God's love is unfailing.
I trust in God's unfailing love for ever and ever.
(Ps. 52:8)

God doesn't change.
Jesus Christ is the same yesterday and today and forever.
(Heb. 13:8)

God is with us.
"Never will I leave you."
(Heb. 13:5)

If you're feeling the intense emotional pain of seeing a loved one sick and hurting…God is still Love.
If you're feeling stressed and overwhelmed by the pressures of life…God is still Sovereign and in control.
If you're grieving the loss of a loved one by death or a broken relationship… God is still with you.
Or maybe you're just feeling down in the dumps…God understands and is still your Prince of Peace.

The book of Psalms does a wonderful job modeling praise during the good times and during times of great suffering. I love the book of Psalms because inspired writers expressed their real feelings as they dealt with real-life situations. We can easily identify with the writers as they passionately poured out their hearts to God. The writers were inspired by God to take up the praise no matter what. Here are two examples of many.

*The LORD is my light and my salvation—
whom shall I fear?
(Ps. 27:1)
God is our refuge and strength, an ever-present help in trouble.
(Ps. 46:1)*

Within the 150 psalms, you'll find the writers exalting God for who He is, for what He has done, and for His glorious attributes. You'll find themes of God's deliverance, mercy, forgiveness, love, trust, and more. You can even find Jesus in the book of Psalms! Here are some examples of inspired words written about Jesus's suffering on the cross before He was even born.

*A band of evil men has encircled me,
they have pierced my hands and my feet.
(Ps. 22:16)*

*They divide my garments among them and cast lots for my clothing.
(Ps. 22:18)*

Praise is a powerful spiritual warfare weapon. The enemy can't stand it when we praise the One True God. Why? Because satan despises the truth and works to steal and twist it. God's Word tells us that satan *"...is a liar and the father of lies"* (John 8:44). The truth is, God is God, and God is the Winner! Praising God through faith in Jesus Christ is empowered by the Holy Spirit and...

makes the enemy shutter,
breaks the chains of oppression,
ushers in the work of God,
brings about inner peace,
puts things in perspective,
helps us remember our blessings,
reminds us of who we are in Christ Jesus,
gives us a sense of well-being,
and revives our souls.

The power of praise is evident throughout the Bible. One example is when Paul and Silas were in prison and decided to praise God and pray. *About midnight Paul and Silas were praying and singing hymns to God, and the other prisoners were listening to them. Suddenly there was such a violent earthquake that the foundations of the prison were shaken. At once all the prison doors flew open, and everybody's chains came loose (Acts 16:25-26).* God chose to release His power. Praise pushes back the schemes of the devil and ushers in the work of God when we...

humbly confess our sins,
accept in faith Jesus as Lord and Savior,
surrender our hearts to the will of God,
have genuine motives,
stand on the promises of God's Word,
and choose to trust in God alone.

Praising God can raise us above life's deepest struggles and pain. As we take up the praise and keep our eyes on Jesus, we find ourselves drawing closer to Him. As a result, our faith is strengthened, and we're empowered to look to Him for everything. He is everything we need!

Another example of the power of praise and its ability to break the power of the enemy is found in Second Chronicles. The people of Judah were under attack, and King Jehoshaphat... *appointed men to sing to the* LORD *and to praise him for the splendor of his holiness as they went out at the head of the army... As they began to sing and praise, the* LORD *set ambushes against the men of Ammon and Moab and Mount Seir who were invading Judah, and they were defeated (2 Chron. 20:21-22).*

Wow! The praise team *went out at the head of the army.* That says a lot about the importance of praising God first. Praise does make a difference...

before making difficult decisions,
before making requests when we pray,
before worship service,
and before starting our days.

Why does praise make a difference? As we take up the praise, our focus changes from the battle to the Victor. We're reminded that God is God and we're not. The truth resonates, and once again we are reminded that God's power and authority reign over all circumstances. He loves us, and He is able to take care of you, everybody, and everything.

Hallelujah! I love the word "hallelujah," because that's the word the great multitude used to express their praise in His presence, right around the very throne of God.

> *Then a voice came from the throne, saying:*
> *"Praise our God, all you his servants,*
> *you who fear him, both small and great!"*
> *Then I heard what sounded like a great multitude,*
> *like the roar of rushing waters and like loud peals of thunder,*
> *shouting: "Hallelujah! For our Lord God Almighty reigns."*
> *(Rev. 19:5-6)*

The praise and worship in this passage is so magnificent that the writer compares what he hears to *the roar of rushing waters and like loud peals of thunder*. The heavenly praise team is like none other. Can you just imagine what that will sound like? We have so much to look forward to.

Praising God is an act of worship whereby we exalt God and give Him the recognition He deserves. There are many different ways to express our praise that lead to worship. Some of my favorite expressions of praise where we shine for Him, boast in Him, and celebrate Him are:

listening to music,
singing and making music,
praying,
writing,
studying God's Word,
being still before God and listening,
and dancing.

Yet, the ultimate expression of praising God is living a life that makes Jesus look good. In other words, living a life that glorifies God.

Listening to Music

I have a twin sister, and I share that to say I've never really felt alone. It seems like I've always had someone with me, even in my mother's womb! It was very hard for me when Carl was in the hospital, in skilled rehab, and then in a nursing home. He was gone from home a long, long time. Being alone at home was a new thing for me, and I didn't like it. But I love music. I played praise music all through the nights. I would wake up in the night, and I would hear words from a song that spoke right to my circumstance. God comforted me and encouraged me through Christian music. Listening to the truth sung about God's promises is powerful. It helped me to turn my eyes upon Jesus. During those dark, lonely nights, I was able to rest in His peace as I sensed God's presence and realized I was not alone. I felt like God was singing over me. This scripture became a reality for me.

*"The LORD your God is with you,
he is mighty to save.
He will take great delight in you,
he will quiet you with his love,
he will rejoice over you with singing."
(Zeph. 3:17)*

What song is God singing over you?

_____
_____
_____
_____
_____

What words from a song bring you comfort and encouragement?
___
___
___
___
___

What helps you to turn your eyes upon Jesus?
___
___
___
___
___

Singing and Making Music

Something that really touches my heart is when I think about Jesus singing. Jesus sang with His disciples after their last supper together and before He was arrested. They ended their time together singing a hymn of praise! In Matthew 26:30, it says, *When they had sung a hymn, they went out to the Mount of Olives.* Wow! Can you imagine that sound? I bet that was a moment in the lives of the disciples they never forgot.

As much as I love music, you might think I could really belt out a pretty song. Well, I can get the volume, but quality is another story. This was proven to me one morning when I taught Sunday school to three-and four-year-olds. I sang the familiar song "Jesus Loves Me" to the class. After I finished singing (my heart out), one little girl said, "Mrs. Elmer, that's not the way it goes." She then proceeded to sing the song the "way it goes." Sometimes it's hard to hear the truth. From that Sunday on, the CD player became my close friend. In my struggle to decide whether to ever sing again (just kidding), I was reminded through scripture that singing is not about performance. Instead, God looks at our hearts. "*Man looks at the outward appearance, but the* LORD *looks at the heart*" (1 Sam. 16:7). No matter what our singing sounds like, when our hearts are sold out for Jesus, the sound is absolutely beautiful to God. What He thinks is what counts. You CAN sing. So take up the praise! Lift your voice and sing!

Sing and make music in your heart to the Lord,
always giving thanks to God the Father for everything,
in the name of our Lord Jesus Christ. (Eph. 5:19-20)

    The words "*make music in your heart*" remind me of my experience playing in the handbell choir at our church. Keep in mind, I know nothing about music. I don't read music, but I love music. One day when I expressed how I'd like to play in the handbell choir, I was encouraged to do so. My fellow bell ringers were very kind and patient. But needless to say, the songs got harder, and I quickly found out that I was in over my head. I'll never forget that Sunday-morning worship service when I was ringing those bells, and I was on the wrong page and the wrong song! I wanted to quit so badly, but I sensed God whispering, "It's not about your performance." I knew then that God thought the sound was beautiful because He was looking at my heart. I continued making music for a few more months until I heard the Lord whisper in my soul, "You can stop now." It was a hallelujah moment!

    Isn't it amazing that God created us to enjoy sounds? Singing and making music are expressions of praise that can help us remember our Creator. Let's praise God, Our Creator, for His wonderful characteristics!

He loves you. *(Ps. 117:2)*
He is with you. *(Matt. 28:20)*
He strengthens you. *(Isa. 41:10)*
He provides for you. *(Phil. 4:19)*
He protects you. *(Ps. 91:14)*
He gives you rest. *(Matt. 11:28)*
He is for you, not against you. *(Rom. 8:28)*

Today, what characteristic of God do you need to be reminded of?
___
___
___
___
___

What song will you sing as an expression of your praise to God?
___
___
___
___
___

Praying

Praising prayer welcomes the presence of God. Being with Jesus in prayer brings great joy. *"You will fill me with joy in your presence" (Acts 2:28).* I'm learning that joy and prayer go hand and hand. Joy is sensing that everything is going to be OK even when our feelings and circumstances say something different. Praising prayer shifts our focus from the storm to the very nature of God, which leads us to a sense of joy. This inner joy is based on God and His Word. True joy comes from realizing that God is in control and that we can trust Him. God's joy calms us no matter how high the waves or how strong the winds. This sense of joy leads us to prayers of praise.

Prayer is simply communicating with God. Our Loving God never gets tired of hearing our praising prayers. It's just like how you and I never get tired of hearing about how much God loves us. Sometimes it can be hard to talk to someone you don't know. It's even harder to praise someone you hardly know. Fortunately, the Bible tells us a lot about the character of God. In the Bible we find out about how Great God is, what He thinks, and how much He loves us. Knowing Him deepens our love for Him and makes it easier to take up the praise. Here are some more characteristics of God, along with supportive scriptures:

Attentive *(1 Pet. 3:12)*
Merciful *(Luke 6:36)*
Awesome *(Ps. 47:2)*
Strong *(Ps. 24:8)*
Speaking God *(Gen. 1)*
Encouraging *(Phil. 1:6)*
Gracious *(Exod. 34:6)*
Almighty *(Ps. 89:8)*
All Knowing *(Matt. 6:8)*
Good *(Ps. 25:8)*
Great *(Ps. 135:5)*

When we meet God in our storms and offer praise in our suffering, the Holy Spirit empowers our praising prayer. We're not the same. Things change when we lay aside ourselves, humbly look toward Jesus, and celebrate Him. I've been blessed to be in a prayer group for many years, and I've seen firsthand God's transforming power. His presence can change…

the tired into the energized,
the oppressed into the uplifted,
worry into a sense of well-being,
the self-centered into the Christ-centered,
the angry into the calm,
grief into hope,
fear into peace,
confusion into truth,
and doubt into trust.

Being with the Holy Spirit of Jesus Christ is transforming. You may be asking, "How can that be?" The answer to that question is that Jesus is the Great I AM. In the book of John, when Jesus was being questioned as to who He really is, this is how He responded: *"I tell you the truth,"* Jesus answered, *"before Abraham was born, I am!" (John 8:58).* "I AM" is in the present tense. He exists today. He is real today. He is powerful today. He gives Himself to us today. His grace is extended to us every day, all day, now. We don't have to fear the future. Our Lord Jesus Christ is everything we need for every moment in our lives. He is the Great I AM.

It always amazes me that God wants us to join Him in His kingdom work. He is so able to do all things on His own, and yet He chooses to include us, and work through the prayers of His people. When we agree with God about the areas of our lives that need to be more like Jesus, and when in faith we stand together wanting God's will, we can expect His power to be released. There is something about God's people coming together in prayer that brings a smile to the face of God.

The more I learn about prayer, the more I realize there's more to learn. The night my life and Carl's life changed drastically, I saw corporate prayer in action. Corporate prayer is when believers unite in faith and pray together. Fellow believers were at our church preparing for a weekend retreat. When the news about Carl's brain bleed and stroke reached them, they immediately began to pray. Family and friends prayed together in the waiting room of the hospital. Many, many people prayed as the news traveled by telephone, text message, and Facebook.

One of the many benefits of corporate prayer is the encouragement given when someone in the group brings you personally to the feet of Jesus in prayer. Hearing others praying for you or knowing that people are praying for you, not only brings encouragement, but also strengthens your faith and reassures you of God's love. I'm thanking God for corporate prayer. I'm still praising Jesus for interceding and being the Warrior King! *The* LORD *is a warrior; the* LORD *is his name (Exod. 15:3)*. But, even if you don't have corporate prayer surrounding you...you are not alone. Jesus is equally present when you pray by yourself or in a group. Jesus is our Great Intercessor. *Christ Jesus, who died—more than that, who was raised to life—is at the right hand of God and is also interceding for us (Rom. 8:34)*.

Sweet hour of prayer! sweet hour of prayer!
that calls me from a world of care,
and bids me at my Father's throne
make all my wants and wishes known.
In seasons of distress and grief,
my soul has often found relief,
and oft escaped the tempter's snare by thy return,
sweet hour of prayer!

Song: "Sweet Hour of Prayer"

Write the names of three people you want to take to Jesus in prayer.
_____
_____
_____
_____
_____

As God's redeemed, we are privileged to praise Him. In a spirit of joy, write a brief prayer praising God.
_____
_____
_____
_____
_____

Writing

In 1996 I began writing to God. I bought a journal, and each day I briefly wrote down something I was thankful for. My reason for doing this was to become more aware of God's presence in my life along with His blessings. Some examples of those journal entries are: "Thank You, Jesus, that I didn't have a headache today," or "Thank You, Lord, that the sun is shining," or "Thank You, Father God, that the traffic going to work kept moving." I called these journals my "thank-you journals." After several journals, my writing took a new direction. I started to write prayers as the Holy Spirit led me. As the next twelve years rolled by, I sensed several times that the Lord was saying to me that He wanted me to put these prayers in a book. I said to the Lord (as if He didn't know), "I don't know how to write and publish a book. I don't have the money. I'm not good at using a computer." After some time, I realized I was looking in the wrong direction; I was looking at me. I decided to refocus. I chose to take a deep breath, step out in faith, and trust Him to guide me. That's just what He did! Step by step, the book fell into place. It has a prayer for each day of the year and is titled *Hallelujah! Amen. It Is Done.* Its subtitle is *Daily Enjoying His Presence*. All glory to Him!

As the years passed and I continued writing, I noticed that my writing was once again taking a new direction. The Holy Spirit created in me such a passion for praise. I remember waking up in the middle of the night sensing that the Lord woke me, but I didn't know why. When I asked, "Lord, what is it? Why did You wake me?" the word that the Lord whispered into my heart was "Praise!" I sensed that something was happening in the heavenly realm. *For our struggle is not against flesh and blood, but against the rulers, against the authorities, against the powers of this dark world and against the spiritual forces of evil in the heavenly realms (Eph. 6:12).* Praising God is kingdom work. Father God is delighted when we pray. He chooses to work through the prayers of His children. I got my pen and journal out and began writing down my praise of God from A to Z.

Father God, You are...

<u>A</u>ll Sufficient
<u>B</u>eautiful Savior
<u>C</u>aring
<u>D</u>eliverer
<u>E</u>ncourager

<u>F</u>aithful <u>F</u>ather
<u>G</u>reat <u>G</u>od
<u>H</u>ope for the <u>H</u>opeless
<u>I</u> AM
<u>J</u>oy-Giver
<u>K</u>ing of <u>K</u>ings
<u>L</u>ove Forevermore
<u>M</u>iracle Worker
<u>N</u>one Like You
<u>O</u>ne and <u>O</u>nly
<u>P</u>rince of <u>P</u>eace
<u>Q</u>uick to Help
<u>R</u>uler
<u>S</u>trong
<u>T</u>otally Holy
<u>U</u>tmost and <u>U</u>pright
<u>V</u>ictorious One
<u>W</u>arrior King
e<u>X</u>cellent and e<u>X</u>alted One
<u>Y</u>ahweh
<u>Z</u>ealous God

    The Holy Spirit of God is such a Wonderful and Patient Teacher. For some, writing doesn't come easy. Our minds race with thoughts like "I can't spell," "I have trouble expressing myself," and "It takes too much time." But with God, writing is not about perfection. Instead, writing is about drawing closer to God and enjoying your relationship with Him. Misspelled words don't bother God. He understands what you say. I'm a student of Jesus Christ. Learning and growing is a lifetime process, and I'm sure not finished. As His student, I can say with confidence and encouragement that…

He never grows tired of repeating instructions;
He gives tests, but never with the intention of seeing you fail;
He never gets in a hurry;
He loves His students; and
His goal is the very best for you.

I pray that you will begin to express your praise by writing down what you would say to God. Expressing your praise in writing is a strong weapon against worry and fear. On those days when praise seems impossible, you can go back to the praise you've written in the past and reread, remember, and rejoice.

Will you praise God for who He is from A to Z?

A_____ B_____
C_____ D_____
E_____ F_____
G_____ H_____
I_____ J_____
K_____ L_____
M_____ N_____
O_____ P_____
Q_____ R_____
S_____ T_____
U_____ V_____
W_____ X_____
Y_____ Z_____

Studying God's Word

I can't stand it when someone lies to me. The biggest reason that I hate lying so much is that, for many years, I believed the lies of the enemy, and I didn't even know it. Whispered lies like "you can't change" and "you'll always be a worrier." I used to worry a lot. Oftentimes my thoughts would begin with "what if." I felt powerless. At that point in my life, I remember being afraid to read the Bible. I worried that I would read something that would scare me! I was confused about God's grace and forgiveness. I needed to know more about Jesus and who I am because of my faith in Him. I didn't know the truth found in the pages of the Bible. Looking back, it's no wonder I felt powerless and wondered where the joy and peace were in my life. In the years that followed, God used the birth of my two sons, my mother, counseling, and godly people to bring me to the point where I wanted to know the truth from God's perspective. I began my search for the truth. I decided to open, read, and study the Bible.

As I studied God's Word, I couldn't get over how many times Jesus said the words, "I tell you the truth." And when Jesus was taken before Pilate, Jesus told him, "...*I came into the world, to testify to the truth*" *(John 18:37)*. As I studied God's Word, the Holy Spirit began to replace lies with the truth. Over the years, God changed my thinking. Step by step, day by day, God replaced anxious thoughts with the truth of His Word.

I can't get over how the Bible is absolutely remarkable! It was written so long ago, but today it's still a bestseller. The Bible has sixty-six separate books written over a long period of time by many different people who lived in different places. It's amazing that the Bible is unified and also supports archaeological evidence and historical facts. It's a God thing! Another supernatural aspect of the Bible is that there are so many prophetic truths about Jesus that were written and spoken before they actually happened. A book like this could never have come into existence without the Holy Spirit directing and enabling these people to write the truth. His Word is the voice of truth. God cannot lie. Lying is not in His character. God keeps His Word. God guarantees everything that was written to be accurate. So in faith we choose to believe that the Bible is the living, inspired, and authoritative Word of God. Psalm 33:4 says it best: *For the word of the* LORD *is right and true; he is faithful in all he does.*

Believing God about Jesus and echoing back His very Word with a humble and contrite heart is powerful praise. Having a personal relationship with Jesus and knowing the truth of God's Word makes scriptures a powerful weapon against the enemy. That kind of praise can lift us up and out of the mud and mire of stormy times. Praising God using the scriptures found in the Bible has the transforming power to shape and mold you into that beautiful, free person God created you to be. *For the word of God is living and active. Sharper than any double-edged sword, it penetrates even to dividing soul and spirit, joints and marrow; it judges the thoughts and attitudes of the heart (Heb. 4:12).*

Studying God's Word has enabled me to have peace and joy in the middle of pain and struggles. Now when I begin to fret or gasp about whatever, I'm reminded to run to the truth and the power of His Word and to praise Him who…

produces change,
guides,
gives peace and joy,
comforts,
delivers,
encourages,
and makes satan run.

Here are some whispered lies followed by praises to God that use the truth of His Word.

Here's the lie: You'll always be a worrier.
Here's the truth: *Therefore, if anyone is in Christ, he is a new creation; the old has gone, the new has come! (2 Cor. 5:17)*

Here's the lie: You're too scared.
Here's the truth: *When I am afraid, I will trust in you. In God, whose word I praise, in God I trust; I will not be afraid. (Ps. 56:3-4)*

Here's the lie: You can't go on much longer. It's just too hard.
Here's the truth: *So do not fear, for I am with you; do not be dismayed, for I am your God. I will strengthen you and help you; I will uphold you with my righteous right hand. (Isa. 41:10)*

Here's the lie: You're alone.
Here's the truth: *"Never will I leave you; never will I forsake you" (Heb. 13:5).*

When we make the decision to choose Jesus as our Savior and the Lord of our lives, His Holy Spirit lives within us. The Holy Spirit helps us understand what God means in the Bible. Spending time studying God's Word is an expression of praise. When we focus our time on God and seek to know Him more, that's taking up the praise! As we stay in the Word, our faith is strengthened, and we can praise God with confidence in any circumstance, saying, "God is Sovereign, Faithful, and True."

What is the lie you refuse to believe?

_____
_____
_____
_____
_____

Now write the truth of God's Word.

_____
_____
_____
_____
_____

Being Still Before God and Listening

God is a speaking God! He wants a real, "in joy" relationship with each one of us. God knows that a vibrant, close, growing relationship needs good communication. Listening as well as speaking makes healthy communication. I can't get over how relational God is. He wants to be with you. He wants you to enjoy His presence. More than anything else, He wants a personal relationship with you through Jesus. "For God so loved the world that he gave his one and only Son, that whoever believes in him shall not perish but have eternal life" (John 3:16).

Therefore, it's natural for God to speak. The Bible gives us many accounts of God speaking, such as...

in dreams (Matt. 1:20-21),
through prophets (Isa. 9:6-7),
in prayer (Acts 12:12-14),

through angels *(Luke 1:19)*,
through miracles *(Exod. 14:21-22)*,
in a burning bush *(Exod. 3:2-4)*,
in visions *(Acts 10:9-16)*,
and many more ways.

What's exciting is that God still speaks today, and we can hear Him! Jesus said so. *"My sheep listen to my voice; I know them, and they follow me" (John 10:27)*. The Holy Spirit can place a thought in your mind or an impression on your heart so strong that it's like hearing Him speak. But keep in mind that God can speak to us any time and in any way He chooses. We cannot put God in a box. He is God, and He still speaks to us today through…

scripture,
prayer,
circumstances,
music,
children and adults,
nature,
visions and dreams,
events,
thoughts,
and sermons.

Years ago when I heard people say that God spoke to them, I thought, "Really?" But as I got to know God more through Bible study, I found out yes, really! God does speak. You might be asking, like I did, "How in the world do you listen to God?" What I've found to be true is that talking to God and asking for things comes a lot easier than being still before God and listening. I want to make it very clear that I'm certainly not an expert listener. But it's true; the more you get to know God and seek His truth, the easier it is to recognize Him.

Throughout the years of seeking God's voice, I've missed it, got it right, and got it wrong. But I've found that the following things help me tune in and listen:

<u>Be Still</u>. Take your position by slowing down and being quiet. Humbly come before God and agree with Him about the areas of your life where you need to be more like Jesus. Praise God for being Merciful and Gracious toward you.

Thank Jesus for dying for your sins. *But Jesus often withdrew to lonely places and prayed (Luke 5:16).*

<u>Invite and Ask</u>. Invite the Holy Spirit to come and guide you to the truth. With the Bible in hand, ask Him to put His words in your thoughts and upon your heart as you read the Bible and listen. *Guide me in your truth and teach me, for you are God my Savior, and my hope is in you all day long (Ps. 25:5).*

<u>Pray</u>. Make your requests. "*Ask and it will be given to you; seek and you will find; knock and the door will be opened to you*" *(Matt. 7:7).*

<u>Be Aware</u>. Watch and be observant. Be aware of what you're hearing in sermons, in songs of worship, in scriptures, and from godly friends. *Let the wise listen and add to their learning... (Prov. 1:5).*

<u>Wait on God</u>. Giving God time is a form of surrender and an act of trust. *I wait for the LORD, my soul waits, and in his word I put my hope (Ps. 130:5).*

<u>Test</u>. Knowing and studying the Bible is vital when discerning if God has spoken. If you sense that you've heard from God, then it's important that you take what you've heard and see if it lines up with the truth of God's written Word. God will not say something to you that is not true. Therefore, the Bible is the best way to test to see if what you're hearing with your "spiritual ears" is from God. We can get confused, and our hearts can deceive us. So if what we're listening to doesn't line up with God's written Word, we should dismiss it and move on. *Test everything. Hold on to the good (1 Thess. 5:21).*

<u>Rejoice</u>. Even if you've missed it, got it right, or got it wrong, keep listening, because the more you seek God's voice, the better you'll be able to hear Him. Rejoice! Listening to God is a joy! *Rejoice in the Lord always. I will say it again: Rejoice! (Phil. 4:4).*

In the stillness of early morning, while still in bed, God placed the word "always" in my mind. I got up and wrote the word "always" in my journal along with a prayer thanking God for His love and for always being with me. It's fun to see how God confirms what He says. A few days later I received a card from a friend, and the words on the card were, "God Is Always With You." Then early one morning I woke up to the lyrics of a song on the radio reminding me of God's unfailing love and the fact that He's always with me. Wow! God is real! With confidence, I knew I was not alone, and God was saying...

*"And surely I am with you always,
to the very end of the age." (Matt. 28:20)*

*It always protects, always trusts,
always hopes, always perseveres. Love never fails.
(1 Cor. 13:7-8)*

I was able to rejoice knowing that I had heard from God. Being reminded of His love and faithfulness encouraged me *and gave me a firm place to stand (Ps. 40:2)*. His powerful words enabled me to face challenges that were way too big for me. In the difficult days that followed, I had to deliberately choose each day to turn my eyes upon Jesus. With Him, I was able to walk on water by joyfully enduring the suffering.

I will never ever forget when God spoke to me through my two-and-a-half-year-old grandson. My husband's future looked very grim after his brain bleed and stroke. My heart was broken, and the storm was raging. In a way that a young child would understand, my daughter-in-law shared with my grandson that his "Pops" was sick. Without hesitating my grandson said, "Jesus loves Pops. Jesus helps Pops feel better." After hearing those words, a sense of well-being filled my heart. I knew God was speaking through this precious child. Even though my circumstances didn't change, I knew the battle was God's, not mine. God gave me a needed reminder that with His help, Carl and I could ride the waves of this raging storm. There's no greater joy than knowing that you've heard from God.

Cultivating an awareness of God's voice requires time and discipline on our part. Believe me, I'm still cultivating this listening awareness, but I can assure you that it's worth it. You won't regret your time spent with Jesus. You'll find yourself praising God and looking forward to being still before Him and listening.

God still speaks today in many different ways. How does God speak to you?
_____
_____
_____
_____
_____

What has God said to you?
_____
_____
_____
_____
_____

Dancing

*There is a time for everything,
and a season for every activity under heaven:*

*a time to weep and a time to laugh,
a time to mourn and a time to dance.
(Eccles. 3:1, 4)*

I love to dance. I'm not good at it, but I sure love to dance. Carl is a very good dancer. I believe that some day we will dance again. Even now in this season of weeping and mourning, I can still dance. You can dance too. Dancing is a celebratory response to Jesus. *You turned my wailing into dancing* (Ps. 30:11).

Years ago I heard someone refer to suffering as a blessing. I thought to myself, "How can that be?" Over the years, I've been seeking to understand from God's perspective how suffering could be a blessing. I sure wish that there were no such thing as suffering, but the bottom line is that we live in a fallen world. We are encouraged in Romans 5, which says that even in our suffering we can live in joy because suffering is not meaningless. God has a purpose for suffering. It makes us...

better,
patient,
persevering,
hopeful,
stronger,
and more like Jesus.

Here's where the dancing comes in. God's Word also says, *For our light and momentary troubles are achieving for us an eternal glory that far outweighs them all (2 Cor. 4:17).* Praise God! Our suffering is temporary. Someday there will be no more suffering! The best is yet to come. Eternal life through Jesus Christ is forevermore. Wow! Let's take up the praise and let Jesus lift our heads and wash away our tears.

Come as you are, even in your suffering. Let Jesus take you to the next step in this dance called life. This dance is not a typical dance that requires movement of your feet and arms. Instead, it requires childlike trust and a laser-like focus on the Leader of the Dance. A childlike trust enables you to rest in His arms. The laser-like focus on Him enables you to live beyond the suffering.

Jesus will never lead you in the wrong direction.
He will guide you step by step.
He will hold you tight.
His embrace is everlasting.
His love is unconditional.
His eyes of grace will ease your pain.

*Turn your eyes upon Jesus,
look full in His wonderful face,
and the things of earth
will grow strangely dim
in the light of His glory and grace.*

Song: "Turn Your Eyes Upon Jesus"

Celebrate Jesus and Dance

Father God, I praise You for being my Joy-Giver.
When I let Jesus lead and rest in His embrace, there is great joy.
Even in my brokenness, I am held together and carried step by step.
Help me to keep my eyes on You.
When I start to look at myself and other things around me, take Your hand and turn my face toward You.
Draw me closer to You and help me to trust Your direction.
I want to live my life like a dance, following Your lead.
Thank You for the joy of being in Your presence.

We can live our lives like a dance when we keep our eyes on Jesus. What can easily take your eyes off Him?

_____
_____
_____
_____
_____

How will you celebrate Jesus today?

_____
_____
_____
_____
_____

Standing Firm

He set my feet on a rock and gave me
a firm place to stand.
He put a new song in my mouth,
a hymn of praise to our God.
(Ps. 40:2-3)

During this difficult season for my husband and me, many times I've been asked the question, "How are YOU doing?" My response used to be, "I'm hanging in there." When my pastor heard my answer, he smiled and encouraged me to respond to that question by saying, "I'm standing firm." He added, "We can't hang on in our own strength. We'll end up letting go and falling, but with God we can stand firm." After pondering what he said, I asked the Lord, "What does it look like to stand firm?"

I'd like to encourage you by sharing some of my personal experiences as God is teaching me and showing me what it looks like to stand firm. The first thing God showed me was that He is God and is in control. I saw the sovereignty of God through the promptness of the first responders, through the ambulance ride in rush hour traffic, and through prayers. As I walked into the recovery room to see my husband for the first time after his surgery, the fact that God is God was so vividly displayed in front of me. Only God could give the knowledge, compassion, and strength I saw coming from the doctors, nurses, and medicines. The thought came to my mind, "Know that I AM God." I immediately was reminded of the scripture in Psalm 46:10: *"Be still, and know that I am God."* I stood there in stillness, knowing I was standing there only by the power of Christ.

In the days that followed, God continued to teach and show me that He uses other people to help us stand firm. God's care and love was reflected through the people He sent to help me. I was not alone.

Family and friends were with me during my husband's surgeries.
Many, many people prayed for us.
People brought us food.
Money was given to us for gas and groceries.

The grass was cut with no charge.
Cards of encouragement came at just the right time.
Every week, our elderly neighbor took our garbage can to the end of our driveway for pickup.

God is teaching me that strength comes when I choose to roll hardships over onto His shoulders. During the difficult days of Carl's hospital, skilled-rehab, and nursing-home stays, I was amazed how the Lord Jesus gave me physical and emotional strength. I knew I was standing firm in the power of Christ. The scripture from Psalm 40:2 that says, *He set my feet on a rock and gave me a firm place to stand* became a reality. The Lord is continuing to teach me the importance of daily taking my position of standing firm on the Solid Rock, no matter how intense the opposition.

God has given us a powerful picture in the book of Ephesians of what it looks like to stand firm. Those standing firm are symbolically described as wearing the full armor of God.

Stand firm then, with the belt of truth buckled around your waist, with the breastplate of righteousness in place, and with your feet fitted with the readiness that comes from the gospel of peace. In addition to all this, take up the shield of faith, with which you can extinguish all the flaming arrows of the evil one. Take the helmet of salvation and the sword of the Spirit, which is the word of God. And pray in the Spirit on all occasions with all kinds of prayers and requests.
(Eph. 6:14-18)

<u>The person standing firm</u> has, by faith, accepted Jesus as his or her Lord and Savior. That makes me think of the *helmet of salvation* and the *breastplate of righteousness*.

<u>The person standing firm</u> is the one who chooses to walk by faith no matter how things look. That's the *shield of faith*.

<u>The person standing firm</u> is watching and ready to tell people the good news about Jesus and His saving grace. That's the *feet fitted with the readiness that comes from the gospel of peace.*

<u>The person standing firm</u> spends time with Jesus, praising Him, thanking Him, confessing, asking, and listening. That's *all kinds of prayers and requests.*

The person standing firm is reading and studying God's Word. That's like wearing the *belt of truth* and having the *sword of the Spirit*.

Wearing God's armor enables us to live in His power even in the days when we're feeling scared, tired, or alone. Choose to stand firm on what you know to be true, not on your feelings. Knowing God's truth and depending on His strength can keep us upright when our walks are hard and each step is a push. We have hope as we stand firm on the truth of His Word…

You have eternal life through Jesus Christ.
"Salvation is found in no one else, for there is no other name under heaven given to men by which we must be saved."
(Acts 4:12)

He forgives!
If we confess our sins, he is faithful and just and will forgive us our sins and purify us from all unrighteousness.
(1 John 1:9)

He will never leave you!
"Fear not, for I have redeemed you; I have summoned you by name; you are mine. When you pass through the waters,
I will be with you."
(Isa. 43:1-2)

You are loved!
For I am convinced that neither death nor life, neither angels nor demons, neither the present nor the future, nor any powers, neither height nor depth, nor anything else in all creation, will be able to separate us from the love of God that is in Christ Jesus our Lord.
(Rom. 8:38-39)

I praise the Holy Spirit of God for being a Wonderful Teacher. He is Patient, Kind, and All Knowing. I love being His student. He is continuing to teach me and show me what it looks like to daily stand firm. Choosing to stand firm in the power of Jesus day by day is living a life that glorifies God. As we choose to stand firm, our lives become the ultimate expression of praise. Wow! I sure hope when I'm asked that question again—"How are YOU doing?"—I'll say with gusto, "I'm standing firm."

Which pieces of God's armor do you wear?
_____
_____
_____
_____
_____

What is your response to the question, "How are YOU doing?"
_____
_____
_____
_____
_____

Write a scripture that gives you hope and helps you to stand firm.
_____
_____
_____
_____
_____

One Tiny Tick of the Clock

*For our light and momentary troubles are achieving for us
an eternal glory that far outweighs them all.
So we fix our eyes not on what is seen, but on what is unseen.
For what is seen is temporary, but what is unseen is eternal.
(2 Cor. 4:17-18)*

I can't get over how fast life is. Life here on earth is extremely short when compared to eternity. Our lives on earth are like one tiny tick of the clock. Comparing my life to one tiny tick of the clock in eternity makes me value every moment here on earth. I want to live life according to what really matters and the purpose for which I was created. James 4:14 describes us as a mist. *You are a mist that appears for a little while and then vanishes.* Webster's Dictionary defines eternity as "endless time."

I have discovered that when trials come unexpectedly and life on earth is hard, keeping an eternal perspective is not easy but is very important. It's so easy to look at the here and now and to lose sight of the fact that *...the gift of God is eternal life in Christ Jesus our Lord (Rom. 6:23)*. God's Word is our lifeline. He keeps His Word. We trust Him for what He's already said. He is Faithful and True. We expect that what He has promised will happen; that's keeping the eternal perspective! Even though we're not home in heaven, we choose to look to Jesus and walk in the victory NOW! Why? Because we have the hope of eternal life, which is forever living life with a personal relationship with Jesus… right now and later in heaven.

Have you ever wondered what eternal life in heaven is like? Some people don't like to talk about heaven. I guess that's because our physical bodies have to die first. But heaven is a great place, and there's lots of celebrating going on. Heaven is definitely a place where God is. It's a fun place to be, and God doesn't want us to miss what He has prepared for us. Jesus said, *"In my Father's house are many rooms; if it were not so, I would have told you. I am going there to prepare a place for you" (John 14:2)*. God has a special place prepared for those who have placed their faith in Jesus. Wow! I can't imagine how fantastic that place is going to be. We have lots to look forward to. "*No eye has seen, no ear has heard, no mind has conceived what God has prepared for those who love him*" *(1 Cor. 2:9)*. The best is yet to come!

We learn some exciting things about heaven from scripture. Heaven is our home and *...our citizenship is in heaven (Phil. 3:20)*. We'll have new bodies too—strong, healthy, vibrant bodies. There will be no more physical limitations, disabilities, or sickness of any kind. There will be no more emotional or physical scars. Everything will be made new. The Bible says, "*He will wipe every tear from their eyes. There will be no more death or mourning or crying or pain, for the old order of things has passed away*" *(Rev. 21:4)*. We'll get to see loved ones who placed their trust in Jesus as their Lord and Savior. In heaven we'll understand things, so save up all your questions. We'll be completely safe, too, and totally protected in heaven. We'll have something to do. We won't be bored. You'll be rewarded in heaven for your faithfulness and obedience. The Bible says we have an inheritance! *Whatever you do, work at it with all your heart, as working for the Lord, not for men, since you know that you will receive an inheritance from the Lord as a reward (Col. 3:23-24)*. People are having a good time in heaven celebrating Jesus. *Then I heard every creature in heaven and on earth and under the earth and on the sea, and all that is in them, singing: "To him who sits on the throne and to the Lamb be praise and honor and glory and power, for ever and ever!" (Rev. 5:13)*. I'm looking forward to being on the praise team in heaven. There's nothing in heaven that will separate us from our Loving God. We don't want to miss heaven!

Sing the wondrous love of Jesus; sing His mercy and His grace.
In the mansions bright and blessed He'll prepare for us a place.
When we all get to heaven, what a day of rejoicing that will be!
When we all see Jesus, we'll sing and shout the victory!
Song: "When We All Get to Heaven"

So how do we get to heaven? We have to make a deliberate choice to be with God in heaven. We must RSVP. Our Heavenly Father eagerly waits for your response to take hold of Jesus's hand and walk with Him now, all the way home. Jesus extended His hand of grace to you, to me, and to the whole world at the cross. *For it is by grace you have been saved, through faith—and this not from yourselves, it is the gift of God—not by works, so that no one can boast (Eph. 2:8-9)*. When you place your hand in Jesus's hand, you're saying, "I believe you died for my sins. Forgive me and turn me away from my sins. I believe you are alive. I want to follow You all the days of my life." God writes your name in His family book, and you become citizens of heaven!

Jesus is the Indescribable Gift, given to us by God, to restore a relationship with Him. Therefore...

> Let us praise Jesus, the Victorious Winner!
> He overcame sin and death!
> He rose from the dead!
> The tomb was empty!
> He publicly defeated satan!
> Jesus is alive!
> He's coming back soon!

With God's help, let's take up the praise and walk on water with Jesus!

What is it about heaven that will help you keep an eternal perspective?

___
___
___
___
___

When comparing your life to one tiny tick of the clock in eternity, what really matters to you?

___
___
___
___
___

Seven Days of Praise

"Hallelujah! For our Lord God Almighty reigns. Let us rejoice and be glad and give him glory!"
(Rev. 19:6-7)

I've been journaling for a long time. It helps me become more aware of God's presence in my life and of His faithfulness. The journal is my place where I come to meet with Jesus. It's a place we enjoy fellowship together. Journaling is simply a tool for developing a deeper, growing relationship with Jesus.

I encourage you to try journaling in any way that best reflects you. There are a variety of different ways you can journal. Some days you might want to just write down how you're feeling. At other times you may want to write some words to a song that you sensed the Holy Spirit brought to your attention. Other days you might write down a familiar scripture that came to your mind.

My favorite way to journal is to start with a couple of sentences praising God for a specific attribute of His. Then after reading the Bible or a devotional, if the Holy Spirit brings certain scriptures to my attention, I write them down. Looking back over that journal entry is like reading a conversation between two friends. God's Word is alive and fresh each day, and it can speak right to your circumstance. The following is an example of an entry:

<u>Me</u>: I praise You, Father God, for being Sovereign and in control. I dedicate this day to You in thanksgiving and praise. Thank You for everything. I know You are making good from my suffering and situation because You said so in Your Word.

<u>God's Word</u>: *And we know that in all things God works for the good of those who love him, who have been called according to his purpose.*
(Rom. 8:28)

<u>Me</u>: I love You.

<u>God's Word</u>: *...your love stands firm forever. (Ps. 89:2)*

Song: *How marvelous! How wonderful!*
And my song shall ever be:
How marvelous! How wonderful is my
Savior's love for me!
Song: "I Stand Amazed in the Presence"

One morning in my journal, I wrote, "Father God, all this is getting too hard. I'm feeling overwhelmed and oppressed. What should I do?" Immediately the words "seven days of praise" entered my mind. That day became the first day of seven days of praise. Praise is a powerful weapon against the enemy's attempt to push us under. As the days passed and I continued to praise God for who He is, the heaviness of my situation lifted. Even when the intensity of the storm rises, praising God enables us to…

endure in joy,
look beyond the troubled waters,
live beyond our capabilities,
and rise above our circumstances.
That's walking on water!

If you're in a storm; if you're tired, scared, and feeling like you're going under; and if you don't know what to do next, take up seven days of praise. Even if you're not in a storm and life is going pretty smoothly, will you begin to praise God for seven days? To praise is a discipline that trains you to turn your eyes upon Jesus. If we daily praise God even when things are going well, then when the storm comes, we'll be ready to stand firm and walk on water. The following seven pages are designed to encourage you to begin your seven days of praise. The format for each day is the same:

scripture,
statement,
take up the praise,
and song.

My prayer is for you to experience the power of praise through Jesus Christ. I pray you will place your hand in Jesus's hand and find yourself living beyond your own capabilities and rising above your circumstances. May you continue to look up and trust Jesus in the stormy days as well as the sunny days. I pray that you will continue to praise God long after seven days. As you live a life of praise, may others see Jesus in you. Together, let's take up the praise and experience the joy of walking on water with Jesus. Hopefully...*Many will see and fear and put their trust in the* LORD *(Ps. 40:3)*.

Turn your eyes upon Jesus,
look full in His wonderful face,
and the things of earth
will grow strangely dim
in the light of His glory and grace.

Song: "Turn Your Eyes Upon Jesus"

Day 1

Scripture:
Why are you downcast, O my soul? Why so disturbed within me? Put your hope in God, for I will yet praise him, my Savior and my God. (Ps. 42:5-6)

When the storm continues and the pain hasn't gone away, You are still worthy of all praise! I choose to look at You and not myself.

<u>Take Up the Praise!</u> (Write your praise in the space below.)
_____
_____
_____
_____
_____
_____
_____

*When peace, like a river, attendeth my way,
when sorrows like sea billows roll;
whatever my lot, Thou hast taught me to say,
It is well, it is well with my soul.*

*It is well with my soul,
It is well with my soul,
it is well, it is well with my soul.*

Song: "It Is Well With My Soul"

Day 2

Scripture:
Praise the LORD, *O my soul;*
all my inmost being, praise his holy name. (Ps. 103:1)

I choose to praise God for who He is.

<u>Take Up the Praise!</u> (Write your praise in the space below.)

_____
_____
_____
_____
_____
_____
_____
_____

Holy, holy, holy! Lord God Almighty!
Early in the morning our song shall rise to Thee.
Holy, holy, holy! Merciful and mighty,
God in three persons, blessed Trinity!

Song: "Holy, Holy, Holy! Lord God Almighty"

Day 3

Scripture:
I will sing to the LORD all my life; I will sing praise to my God as long as I live. (Ps. 104:33)

When the days are long and the storm lasts longer than expected, I will trust my Jesus. I want my life to be a song of praise!

Take Up the Praise! (Write your praise in the space below.)
_____
_____
_____
_____
_____
_____
_____

*Amazing grace! How sweet the sound
that saved a wretch like me!
I once was lost, but now am found;
was blind, but now I see.*

*'Twas grace that taught my heart to fear,
and grace my fears relieved;
how precious did that grace appear
the hour I first believed.*

Song: "Amazing Grace"

Day 4

Scripture:
I will give thanks to the LORD *because of his righteousness and will sing praise to the name of the* LORD *Most High. (Ps. 7:17)*

I come with a grateful heart. Thank You, Lord, for loving me and caring for me.

<u>Take Up the Praise!</u> (Write your praise in the space below.)
_____
_____
_____
_____
_____
_____
_____

Be not dismayed whate'er betide,
God will take care of you;
beneath His wings of love abide,
God will take care of you.

God will take care of you,
through every day, o'er all the way;
He will take care of you,
God will take care of you.

Song: "God Will Take Care of You"

Day 5

Scripture:
Sing the glory of his name; make his praise glorious! Say to God, "How awesome are your deeds! So great is your power that your enemies cringe before you." (Ps. 66:2-3)

Even though we may be taken by surprise, God is never taken by surprise. I stand in awe of You.

Take Up the Praise! (Write your praise in the space below.)
_____
_____
_____
_____
_____
_____
_____

*Standing on the promises of Christ my King,
through eternal ages let His praises ring;
glory in the highest, I will shout and sing,
standing on the promises of God.*

*Standing, standing,
standing on the promises of God my Savior;
standing, standing,
I'm standing on the promises of God.*

Song: "Standing on the Promises"

Day 6

Scripture:
I will praise you, O Lord my God, with all my heart; I will glorify your name forever. For great is your love toward me. (Psalm 86:12-13)

Jesus truly loves me. His love is unconditional, unfailing, and forever.

<u>Take Up the Praise!</u> (Write your praise in the space below.)

_____
_____
_____
_____
_____
_____
_____
_____

Jesus loves me! This I know,
for the Bible tells me so.
Little ones to Him belong;
they are weak, but He is strong.

Yes, Jesus loves me!
Yes, Jesus loves me!
Yes, Jesus loves me!
The Bible tells me so.

Song: "Jesus Loves Me"

Day 7

Scripture:
Let everything that has breath praise the LORD. *Praise the* LORD.
(Ps. 150:6)

You are worthy of all my praise.

<u>Take Up the Praise!</u> (Write your praise in the space below.)
_____
_____
_____
_____
_____
_____
_____

Be thou my vision,
O Lord of my heart;
naught be all else to me,
save that thou art.
Thou my best thought,
by day or by night,
waking or sleeping,
thy presence my light.

Song: "Be Thou My Vision" (verse one)

Appendix

Song: "Blessed Assurance"
Words: Fanny Crosby, 1873
Music: Phoebe P. Knapp, 1873

Song: "Turn Your Eyes Upon Jesus"
Words and Music: Helen H. Lemmel, 1922

Song: "Sweet Hour of Prayer"
Words: William Walford, 1845
Music: William B. Bradbury, 1861

Song: "When We All Get to Heaven"
Words: Eliza E. Hewitt, 1898
Music: Emily D. Wilson, 1898

Song: "I Stand Amazed in the Presence"
Words and Music: Charles H. Gabriel, 1905

Song: "It Is Well With My Soul"
Words: Horatio G. Spafford, 1873
Music: Philip P. Bliss, 1876

Song: "Holy, Holy, Holy! Lord God Almighty"
Words: Reginald Heber, 1826
Music: John B. Dykes, 1861

Song: "Amazing Grace"
Words: John Newton 1779
Music: 19th cent. USA melody; harm. by Edwin O. Excell, 1900 New Britain, James P. Carrell and David S. Clayton, 1831

Song: "God Will Take Care of You"
Words: Civilla D. Martin, 1904
Music: W. Stillman Martin, 1905

Song: "Standing On the Promises"
Words and Music: R. Kelso Carter, 1886

Song: "Jesus Loves Me"
Words: Anna B. Warner, 1860
Music: William B. Bradbury, 1862

Song: "Be Thou My Vision" (verse one)
Words: trans. Mary E. Byrne, 1905; versed by Eleanor H. Hull, 1912
Music: trad. Irish melody; harm. by Carlton R. Young, 1963

Made in the USA
Lexington, KY
03 May 2015